HAL•LEONARD

Jazz Play-Along®

k and CD for B♭, E♭, C and Bass Clef Instruments

Volume
166

Arranged and Produced
by Mark Taylor

ornette COLEMAN

BOOK

CD

Cover photo © Michael Ochs Archives/Getty Images

ISBN 978-1-4584-9124-4

HAL•LEONARD®
CORPORATION
7777 W. BLUEMOUND RD. P.O. BOX 13819 MILWAUKEE, WI 53213

Visit Hal Leonard Online at
www.halleonard.com

ORNETTE COLEMAN

Volume 166

Arranged and Produced by Mark Taylor

Featured Players:

Graham Breedlove–Trumpet
John Desalme–Saxes
Tony Nalker–Piano
Regan Brough–Bass
Todd Harrison–Drums

Recorded at Bias Studios, Springfield, Virginia
Bob Dawson, Engineer

HOW TO USE THE CD:

Each song has <u>two</u> tracks:

1) Split Track/Melody

Woodwind, Brass, Keyboard, and **Mallet Players** can use this track as a learning tool for melody style and inflection.

Bass Players can learn and perform with this track – remove the recorded bass track by turning down the volume on the LEFT channel.

Keyboard and **Guitar Players** can learn and perform with this track – remove the recorded piano part by turning down the volume on the RIGHT channel.

2) Full Stereo Track

Soloists or **Groups** can learn and perform with this accompaniment track with the RHYTHM SECTION only.

THE BLESSING

BY ORNETTE COLEMAN

C VERSION

CHIPPIE

C VERSION

BY ORNETTE COLEMAN

THE DISGUISE

BY ORNETTE COLEMAN

C VERSION

TEARS INSIDE

BY ORNETTE COLEMAN

C VERSION

JAYNE

BY ORNETTE COLEMAN

CD

7 : SPLIT TRACK/MELODY
8 : FULL STEREO TRACK

C VERSION

REJOICING

BY ORNETTE COLEMAN

C VERSION

TURNAROUND

BY ORNETTE COLEMAN

C VERSION

WHEN WILL THE BLUES LEAVE

BY ORNETTE COLEMAN

C VERSION

THE BLESSING

BY ORNETTE COLEMAN

CD
1 : SPLIT TRACK/MELODY
2 : FULL STEREO TRACK

Bb VERSION

CHIPPIE

BY ORNETTE COLEMAN

Bb VERSION

THE DISGUISE

CD

◆5◆ : SPLIT TRACK/MELODY

◆6◆ : FULL STEREO TRACK

Bb VERSION

BY ORNETTE COLEMAN

Tears Inside

BY ORNETTE COLEMAN

Jayne

BY ORNETTE COLEMAN

CD
- 7 : SPLIT TRACK/MELODY
- 8 : FULL STEREO TRACK

Bb VERSION

REJOICING

BY ORNETTE COLEMAN

CD
9 : SPLIT TRACK/MELODY
10 : FULL STEREO TRACK

Bb VERSION

CD

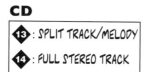
- **13**: SPLIT TRACK/MELODY
- **14**: FULL STEREO TRACK

TURNAROUND

BY ORNETTE COLEMAN

Bb VERSION

WHEN WILL THE BLUES LEAVE

BY ORNETTE COLEMAN

THE BLESSING

BY ORNETTE COLEMAN

Eb VERSION

CHIPPIE

BY ORNETTE COLEMAN

Eb VERSION

THE DISGUISE

BY ORNETTE COLEMAN

Eb VERSION

Tears Inside

BY ORNETTE COLEMAN

Jayne

BY ORNETTE COLEMAN

CD

7 : SPLIT TRACK/MELODY
8 : FULL STEREO TRACK

Eb VERSION

REJOICING

CD
🔹**13** : SPLIT TRACK/MELODY
🔹**14** : FULL STEREO TRACK

Turnaround

BY ORNETTE COLEMAN

Eb VERSION

WHEN WILL THE BLUES LEAVE

BY ORNETTE COLEMAN

THE BLESSING

BY ORNETTE COLEMAN

CHIPPIE

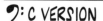

CD
- 3 : SPLIT TRACK/MELODY
- 4 : FULL STEREO TRACK

BY ORNETTE COLEMAN

𝄢: C VERSION

CD

THE DISGUISE

BY ORNETTE COLEMAN

𝄢: C VERSION

Tears Inside

BY ORNETTE COLEMAN

𝄢: C VERSION

CD

Jayne

BY ORNETTE COLEMAN

C VERSION

REJOICING

CD
- ◆ 9 : SPLIT TRACK/MELODY
- ◆ 10 : FULL STEREO TRACK

BY ORNETTE COLEMAN

𝄢: C VERSION

TURNAROUND

BY ORNETTE COLEMAN

WHEN WILL THE BLUES LEAVE

BY ORNETTE COLEMAN

Presenting the Hal Leonard JAZZ PLAY-ALONG SERIES

For use with all B-flat, E-flat, Bass Clef and C instruments, the Jazz Play-Along® Series is the ultimate learning tool for all jazz musicians. With musician-friendly lead sheets, melody cues, and other split-track choices on the included CD, these first-of-a-kind packages help you master improvisation while playing some of the greatest tunes of all time. FOR STUDY, each tune includes a split track with: melody cue with proper style and inflection • professional rhythm tracks • choruses for soloing • removable bass part • removable piano part. FOR PERFORMANCE, each tune also has: an additional full stereo accompaniment track (no melody) • additional choruses for soloing.

1A. MAIDEN VOYAGE/ALL BLUES
00843158 ....$15.99

1. DUKE ELLINGTON
00841644 ....$16.95

2. MILES DAVIS
00841645 ....$16.95

3. THE BLUES
00841646 ....$16.99

4. JAZZ BALLADS
00841691 ....$16.99

5. BEST OF BEBOP
00841689 ....$16.95

6. JAZZ CLASSICS WITH EASY CHANGES
00841690 ....$16.99

7. ESSENTIAL JAZZ STANDARDS
00843000 ....$16.99

8. ANTONIO CARLOS JOBIM AND THE ART OF THE BOSSA NOVA
00843001 ....$16.95

9. DIZZY GILLESPIE
00843002 ....$16.99

10. DISNEY CLASSICS
00843003 ....$16.99

11. RODGERS AND HART FAVORITES
00843004 ....$16.99

12. ESSENTIAL JAZZ CLASSICS
00843005 ....$16.99

13. JOHN COLTRANE
00843006 ....$16.95

14. IRVING BERLIN
00843007 ....$15.99

15. RODGERS & HAMMERSTEIN
00843008 ....$15.99

16. COLE PORTER
00843009 ....$15.95

17. COUNT BASIE
00843010 ....$16.95

18. HAROLD ARLEN
00843011 ....$15.95

19. COOL JAZZ
00843012 ....$15.95

20. CHRISTMAS CAROLS
00843080 ....$14.95

21. RODGERS AND HART CLASSICS
00843014 ....$14.95

22. WAYNE SHORTER
00843015 ....$16.95

23. LATIN JAZZ
00843016 ....$16.95

24. EARLY JAZZ STANDARDS
00843017 ....$14.95

25. CHRISTMAS JAZZ
00843018 ....$16.95

26. CHARLIE PARKER
00843019 ....$16.95

27. GREAT JAZZ STANDARDS
00843020 ....$16.99

28. BIG BAND ERA
00843021 ....$15.99

29. LENNON AND MCCARTNEY
00843022 ....$16.95

30. BLUES' BEST
00843023 ....$15.99

31. JAZZ IN THREE
00843024 ....$15.99

32. BEST OF SWING
00843025 ....$15.99

33. SONNY ROLLINS
00843029 ....$15.95

34. ALL TIME STANDARDS
00843030 ....$15.99

35. BLUESY JAZZ
00843031 ....$16.99

36. HORACE SILVER
00843032 ....$16.99

37. BILL EVANS
00843033 ....$16.95

38. YULETIDE JAZZ
00843034 ....$16.95

39. "ALL THE THINGS YOU ARE" & MORE JEROME KERN SONGS
00843035 ....$15.99

40. BOSSA NOVA
00843036 ....$16.99

41. CLASSIC DUKE ELLINGTON
00843037 ....$16.99

42. GERRY MULLIGAN FAVORITES
00843038 ....$16.99

43. GERRY MULLIGAN CLASSICS
00843039 ....$16.99

44. OLIVER NELSON
00843040 ....$16.95

45. GEORGE GERSHWIN
00103643 ....$24.99

46. BROADWAY JAZZ STANDARDS
00843042 ....$15.99

47. CLASSIC JAZZ BALLADS
00843043 ....$15.99

48. BEBOP CLASSICS
00843044 ....$16.99

49. MILES DAVIS STANDARDS
00843045 ....$16.95

50. GREAT JAZZ CLASSICS
00843046 ....$15.99

51. UP-TEMPO JAZZ
00843047 ....$15.99

52. STEVIE WONDER
00843048 ....$16.99

53. RHYTHM CHANGES
00843049 ....$15.99

54. "MOONLIGHT IN VERMONT" AND OTHER GREAT STANDARDS
00843050 ....$15.99

55. BENNY GOLSON
00843052 ....$15.95

56. "GEORGIA ON MY MIND" & OTHER SONGS BY HOAGY CARMICHAEL
00843056 ....$15.99

57. VINCE GUARALDI
00843057 ....$16.99

58. MORE LENNON AND MCCARTNEY
00843059 ....$16.99

59. SOUL JAZZ
00843060 ....$16.99

60. DEXTER GORDON
00843061 ....$15.95

61. MONGO SANTAMARIA
00843062 ....$15.95

62. JAZZ-ROCK FUSION
00843063 ....$16.99

63. CLASSICAL JAZZ
00843064 ....$14.95

64. TV TUNES
00843065 ....$14.95

65. SMOOTH JAZZ
00843066 ....$16.99

66. A CHARLIE BROWN CHRISTMAS
00843067 ....$16.99

67. CHICK COREA
00843068 ....$15.95

68. CHARLES MINGUS
00843069 ....$16.95

69. CLASSIC JAZZ
00843071 ....$15.99

70. THE DOORS
00843072 ....$14.95

71. COLE PORTER CLASSICS
00843073 ....$14.95

72. CLASSIC JAZZ BALLADS
00843074 ....$15.99

73. JAZZ/BLUES
00843075......$14.95

74. BEST JAZZ CLASSICS
00843076......$15.99

75. PAUL DESMOND
00843077......$16.99

76. BROADWAY JAZZ BALLADS
00843078......$15.99

77. JAZZ ON BROADWAY
00843079......$15.99

78. STEELY DAN
00843070......$15.99

79. MILES DAVIS CLASSICS
00843081......$15.99

80. JIMI HENDRIX
00843083......$16.99

81. FRANK SINATRA – CLASSICS
00843084......$15.99

82. FRANK SINATRA – STANDARDS
00843085......$16.99

83. ANDREW LLOYD WEBBER
00843104......$14.95

84. BOSSA NOVA CLASSICS
00843105......$14.95

85. MOTOWN HITS
00843109......$14.95

86. BENNY GOODMAN
00843110......$15.99

87. DIXIELAND
00843111......$16.99

88. DUKE ELLINGTON FAVORITES
00843112......$14.95

89. IRVING BERLIN FAVORITES
00843113......$14.95

90. THELONIOUS MONK CLASSICS
00841262......$16.99

91. THELONIOUS MONK FAVORITES
00841263......$16.99

92. LEONARD BERNSTEIN
00450134......$15.99

93. DISNEY FAVORITES
00843142......$14.99

94. RAY
00843143......$14.99

95. JAZZ AT THE LOUNGE
00843144......$14.99

96. LATIN JAZZ STANDARDS
00843145......$15.99

97. MAYBE I'M AMAZED*
00843148......$15.99

98. DAVE FRISHBERG
00843149......$15.99

99. SWINGING STANDARDS
00843150......$14.99

100. LOUIS ARMSTRONG
00740423......$16.99

101. BUD POWELL
00843152......$14.99

102. JAZZ POP
00843153......$15.99

**103. ON GREEN DOLPHIN STREET
& OTHER JAZZ CLASSICS**
00843154......$14.99

104. ELTON JOHN
00843155......$14.99

105. SOULFUL JAZZ
00843151......$15.99

106. SLO' JAZZ
00843117......$14.99

107. MOTOWN CLASSICS
00843116......$14.99

108. JAZZ WALTZ
00843159......$15.99

109. OSCAR PETERSON
00843160......$16.99

110. JUST STANDARDS
00843161......$15.99

111. COOL CHRISTMAS
00843162......$15.99

112. PAQUITO D'RIVERA – LATIN JAZZ*
48020662......$16.99

113. PAQUITO D'RIVERA – BRAZILIAN JAZZ*
48020663......$19.99

114. MODERN JAZZ QUARTET FAVORITES
00843163......$15.99

115. THE SOUND OF MUSIC
00843164......$15.99

116. JACO PASTORIUS
00843165......$15.99

117. ANTONIO CARLOS JOBIM – MORE HITS
00843166......$15.99

118. BIG JAZZ STANDARDS COLLECTION
00843167......$27.50

119. JELLY ROLL MORTON
00843168......$15.99

120. J.S. BACH
00843169......$15.99

121. DJANGO REINHARDT
00843170......$15.99

122. PAUL SIMON
00843182......$16.99

123. BACHARACH & DAVID
00843185......$15.99

124. JAZZ-ROCK HORN HITS
00843186......$15.99

126. COUNT BASIE CLASSICS
00843157......$15.99

127. CHUCK MANGIONE
00843188......$15.99

128. VOCAL STANDARDS (LOW VOICE)
00843189......$15.99

129. VOCAL STANDARDS (HIGH VOICE)
00843190......$15.99

130. VOCAL JAZZ (LOW VOICE)
00843191......$15.99

131. VOCAL JAZZ (HIGH VOICE)
00843192......$15.99

132. STAN GETZ ESSENTIALS
00843193......$15.99

133. STAN GETZ FAVORITES
00843194......$15.99

134. NURSERY RHYMES*
00843196......$17.99

135. JEFF BECK
00843197......$15.99

136. NAT ADDERLEY
00843198......$15.99

137. WES MONTGOMERY
00843199......$15.99

138. FREDDIE HUBBARD
00843200......$15.99

139. JULIAN "CANNONBALL" ADDERLEY
00843201......$15.99

140. JOE ZAWINUL
00843202......$15.99

141. BILL EVANS STANDARDS
00843156......$15.99

142. CHARLIE PARKER GEMS
00843222......$15.99

143. JUST THE BLUES
00843223......$15.99

144. LEE MORGAN
00843229......$15.99

145. COUNTRY STANDARDS
00843230......$15.99

146. RAMSEY LEWIS
00843231......$15.99

147. SAMBA
00843232......$15.99

150. JAZZ IMPROV BASICS
00843195......$19.99

151. MODERN JAZZ QUARTET CLASSICS
00843209......$15.99

152. J.J. JOHNSON
00843210......$15.99

154. HENRY MANCINI
00843213......$14.99

155. SMOOTH JAZZ CLASSICS
00843215......$15.99

156. THELONIOUS MONK – EARLY GEMS
00843216......$15.99

157. HYMNS
00843217......$15.99

158. JAZZ COVERS ROCK
00843219......$15.99

159. MOZART
00843220......$15.99

160. GEORGE SHEARING
14041531......$16.99

161. DAVE BRUBECK
14041556......$16.99

162. BIG CHRISTMAS COLLECTION
00843221......$24.99

164. HERB ALPERT
14041775......$16.99

165. GEORGE BENSON
00843240......$16.99

167. JOHNNY MANDEL
00103642......$16.99

168. TADD DAMERON
00103663......$15.99

169. BEST JAZZ STANDARDS
00109249......$19.99

170. ULTIMATE JAZZ STANDARDS
00109250......$19.99

172. POP STANDARDS
00111669......$15.99

174. TIN PAN ALLEY
00119125......$15.99

175. TANGO
00119836......$15.99

176. JOHNNY MERCER
00119838......$15.99

*These CDs do not include split tracks.

1013

Jazz Instruction & Improvisation

BOOKS FOR ALL INSTRUMENTS FROM HAL LEONARD

AN APPROACH TO JAZZ IMPROVISATION
by Dave Pozzi
Musicians Institute Press

Explore the styles of Charlie Parker, Sonny Rollins, Bud Powell and others with this comprehensive guide to jazz improvisation. Covers: scale choices • chord analysis • phrasing • melodies • harmonic progressions • more.
00695135 Book/CD Pack......................................$17.95

THE ART OF MODULATING
FOR PIANISTS AND JAZZ MUSICIANS
by Carlos Salzedo &
Lucile Lawrence
Schirmer

The Art of Modulating is a treatise originally intended for the harp, but this edition has been edited for use by intermediate keyboardists and other musicians who have an understanding of basic music theory. In its pages you will find: table of intervals; modulation rules; modulation formulas; examples of modulation; extensions and cadences; ten fragments of dances; five characteristic pieces; and more.
50490581 ....$19.99

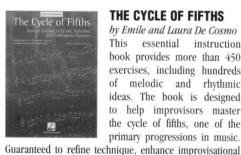

BUILDING A JAZZ VOCABULARY
By Mike Steinel

A valuable resource for learning the basics of jazz from Mike Steinel of the University of North Texas. It covers: the basics of jazz • how to build effective solos • a comprehensive practice routine • and a jazz vocabulary of the masters.
00849911 ....$19.95

THE CYCLE OF FIFTHS
by Emile and Laura De Cosmo

This essential instruction book provides more than 450 exercises, including hundreds of melodic and rhythmic ideas. The book is designed to help improvisors master the cycle of fifths, one of the primary progressions in music. Guaranteed to refine technique, enhance improvisational fluency, and improve sight-reading!
00311114 ....$16.99

THE DIATONIC CYCLE
by Emile and Laura De Cosmo
Renowned jazz educators Emile and Laura De Cosmo provide more than 300 exercises to help improvisors tackle one of music's most common progressions: the diatonic cycle. This book is guaranteed to refine technique, enhance improvisational fluency, and improve sight-reading!
00311115 ....$16.95

EAR TRAINING
by Keith Wyatt,
Carl Schroeder and Joe Elliott
Musicians Institute Press
Covers: basic pitch matching • singing major and minor scales • identifying intervals • transcribing melodies and rhythm • identifying chords and progressions • seventh chords and the blues • modal interchange, chromaticism, modulation • and more.
00695198 Book/2-CD Pack...................................$24.95

EXERCISES AND ETUDES FOR THE JAZZ INSTRUMENTALIST
by J.J. Johnson
Designed as study material and playable by any instrument, these pieces run the gamut of the jazz experience, featuring common and uncommon time signatures and keys, and styles from ballads to funk. They are progressively graded so that both beginners and professionals will be challenged by the demands of this wonderful music.
00842018 Bass Clef Edition $16.95
00842042 Treble Clef Edition $16.95

JAZZOLOGY
THE ENCYCLOPEDIA OF JAZZ THEORY FOR ALL MUSICIANS
by Robert Rawlins and
Nor Eddine Bahha
This comprehensive resource covers a variety of jazz topics, for beginners and pros of any instrument. The book serves as an encyclopedia for reference, a thorough methodology for the student, and a workbook for the classroom.
00311167 ....$19.99

JAZZ THEORY RESOURCES
by Bert Ligon
Houston Publishing, Inc.
This is a jazz theory text in two volumes. **Volume 1 includes**: review of basic theory • rhythm in jazz performance • triadic generalization • diatonic harmonic progressions and analysis • substitutions and turnarounds • and more. **Volume 2 includes**: modes and modal frameworks • quartal harmony • extended tertian structures and triadic superimposition • pentatonic applications • coloring "outside" the lines and beyond • and more.
00030458 Volume 1 ....$39.95
00030459 Volume 2 ....$29.95

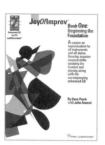

JOY OF IMPROV
by Dave Frank
and John Amaral
This book/CD course on improvisation for all instruments and all styles will help players develop monster musical skills! Book One imparts a solid basis in technique, rhythm, chord theory, ear training and improv concepts. **Book Two** explores more advanced chord voicings, chord arranging techniques and more challenging blues and melodic lines. The CD can be used as a listening and play-along tool.
00220005 Book 1 – Book/CD Pack......................$27.99
00220006 Book 2 – Book/CD Pack......................$26.99

THE PATH TO JAZZ IMPROVISATION
by Emile and Laura De Cosmo
This fascinating jazz instruction book offers an innovative, scholarly approach to the art of improvisation. It includes in-depth analysis and lessons about: cycle of fifths • diatonic cycle • overtone series • pentatonic scale • harmonic and melodic minor scale • polytonal order of keys • blues and bebop scales • modes • and more.
00310904 ....$14.99

THE SOURCE
THE DICTIONARY OF CONTEMPORARY AND TRADITIONAL SCALES
by Steve Barta
This book serves as an informative guide for people who are looking for good, solid information regarding scales, chords, and how they work together. It provides right and left hand fingerings for scales, chords, and complete inversions. Includes over 20 different scales, each written in all 12 keys.
00240885 ....$18.99

21 BEBOP EXERCISES
by Steve Rawlins
This book/CD pack is both a warm-up collection and a manual for bebop phrasing. Its tasty and sophisticated exercises will help you develop your proficiency with jazz interpretation. It concentrates on practice in all twelve keys – moving higher by half-step – to help develop dexterity and range. The companion CD includes all of the exercises in 12 keys.
00315341 Book/CD Pack......................................$17.95

HAL•LEONARD®
CORPORATION
7777 W. BLUEMOUND RD. P.O. BOX 13819 MILWAUKEE, WI 53213

Visit Hal Leonard online at
www.halleonard.com

Prices, contents & availability subject to change without notice.

The Best-Selling Jazz Book of All Time Is Now Legal!

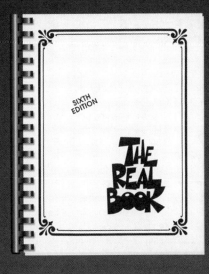

The Real Books are the most popular jazz books of all time. Since the 1970s, musicians have trusted these volumes to get them through every gig, night after night. The problem is that the books were illegally produced and distributed, without any regard to copyright law, or royalties paid to the composers who created these musical masterpieces.

Hal Leonard is very proud to present the first legitimate and legal editions of these books ever produced. You won't even notice the difference, other than all the notorious errors being fixed: the covers and typeface look the same, the song lists are nearly identical, and the price for our edition is even cheaper than the originals!

Every conscientious musician will appreciate that these books are now produced accurately and ethically, benefitting the songwriters that we owe for some of the greatest tunes of all time!

VOLUME 1

00240221	C Edition	$35.00
00240224	B♭ Edition	$35.00
00240225	E♭ Edition	$35.00
00240226	Bass Clef Edition	$35.00
00240292	C Edition 6 x 9	$30.00
00240339	B♭ Edition 6 x 9	$30.00
00451087	C Edition on CD-ROM	$25.00
00240302	A-D CD Backing Tracks	$24.99
00240303	E-J CD Backing Tracks	$24.95
00240304	L-R CD Backing Tracks	$24.95
00240305	S-Z CD Backing Tracks	$24.99
00110604	Book/USB Flash Drive Backing Tracks Pack	$79.99
00110599	USB Flash Drive Only	$50.00

VOLUME 2

00240222	C Edition	$35.50
00240227	B♭ Edition	$35.00
00240228	E♭ Edition	$35.00
00240229	Bass Clef Edition	$35.00
00240293	C Edition 6 x 9	$30.00
00451088	C Edition on CD-ROM	$27.99
00240351	A-D CD Backing Tracks	$24.99
00240352	E-I CD Backing Tracks	$24.99
00240353	J-R CD Backing Tracks	$24.99
00240354	S-Z CD Backing Tracks	$24.99

VOLUME 3

00240233	C Edition	$35.00
00240284	B♭ Edition	$35.00
00240285	E♭ Edition	$35.00
00240286	Bass Clef Edition	$35.00
00240338	C Edition 6 x 9	$30.00
00451089	C Edition on CD-ROM	$29.99

VOLUME 4

00240296	C Edition	$35.00
00103348	B♭ Edition	$35.00
00103349	E♭ Edition	$35.00
00103350	Bass Clef Edition	$35.00

VOLUME 5

00240349	C Edition	$35.00

Also available:

00240264	The Real Blues Book	$34.99
00310910	The Real Bluegrass Book	$29.99
00240137	Miles Davis Real Book	$19.95
00240355	The Real Dixieland Book	$29.99
00240235	The Duke Ellington Real Book	$19.99
00240348	The Real Latin Book	$35.00
00240358	The Charlie Parker Real Book	$19.99
00240331	The Bud Powell Real Book	$19.99
00240313	The Real Rock Book	$35.00
00240323	The Real Rock Book – Vol. 2	$35.00
00240359	The Real Tab Book – Vol. 1	$32.50
00240317	The Real Worship Book	$29.99

THE REAL CHRISTMAS BOOK

00240306	C Edition	$29.99
00240345	B♭ Edition	$29.99
00240346	E♭ Edition	$29.99
00240347	Bass Clef Edition	$29.99
00240431	A-G CD Backing Tracks	$24.99
00240432	H-M CD Backing Tracks	$24.99
00240433	N-Y CD Backing Tracks	$24.99

THE REAL VOCAL BOOK

00240230	Volume 1 High Voice	$35.00
00240307	Volume 1 Low Voice	$35.00
00240231	Volume 2 High Voice	$35.00
00240308	Volume 2 Low Voice	$35.00
00240391	Volume 3 High Voice	$35.00
00240392	Volume 3 Low Voice	$35.00

THE REAL BOOK – STAFF PAPER

00240327	$10.99

HOW TO PLAY FROM A REAL BOOK
FOR ALL MUSICIANS
by Robert Rawlins

00312097	$17.50

Complete song lists online
at www.halleonard.com

Prices, content, and availability subject to change without notice.

HAL•LEONARD®
CORPORATION

7777 W. BLUEMOUND RD. P.O. BOX 13819 MILWAUKEE, WI 53213

1113

ARTIST TRANSCRIPTIONS®

Artist Transcriptions are authentic, note-for-note transcriptions of today's hottest artists in jazz, pop and rock. These outstanding, accurate arrangements are in an easy-to-read format which includes all essential lines. **Artist Transcriptions** can be used to perform, sequence or for reference.